GEDCOM DATA
moving your family tree

by David Hawgood

3rd edition
published by David Hawgood
London, 1999

Contents

This book is dedicated to the memory of my wife's aunt Mrs Lorna Beecham, whose enthusiasm for finding more about her Excell ancestors inspired me.

GEDCOM DATA TRANSFER: moving your family tree
by David Hawgood MA FBCS FSG

This third edition published 1999 by David Hawgood,
26 Cloister Road, Acton, London W3 0DE,
and distributed by Family Tree Magazine,
61 Great Whyte, Ramsey, Huntingdon, Cambs PE17 1HL;
phone 01487 814050, fax 01487 711361.

The second edition was published by David Hawgood in 1994,
the first edition was published by Hawgood Computing Limited in 1991.

ISBN 0 948151 17 X

Typeset by the author using WordPerfect. The text is set in *Times Roman*. Headings are in *Univers*. File listings and screen displays are in *Letter Gothic*. The cover illustration is reproduced from the Dover Publications book *More Silhouettes*.

Printed in England by Parchment (Oxford) Ltd, Crescent Road, Oxford.

ACKNOWLEDGMENTS

I thank Jeanne Bunting, John Bloore and Murray Kennedy for helpful comments on the first edition of this book.

I thank the Family History Department of the Church of Jesus Christ of Latter Day Saints for initiating and producing the GEDCOM standard. All family historians using computers owe them a debt of gratitude for making it possible to transfer information between different computer systems. I should also emphasise that the definitive statements on GEDCOM are the standards published by the Church of Jesus Christ of Latter Day Saints. My book is a commentary, independent of the publishers of the standards.

1. INTRODUCTION

You can use GEDCOM to copy and preserve family tree information. GEDCOM is a method of transferring genealogy data between different computer systems, and different genealogy packages. The GEDCOM standard specifies the structure of an intermediate file. This is a simple file which it is easy to transfer from one computer to another, by moving a floppy disk or by data communications.

Different genealogy packages have different ways of holding information. To make a copy for transfer, one package exports data to a file in the common GEDCOM format. The other package imports the GEDCOM data to its own structure. The transfer includes information about family relationships; GEDCOM data is lineage-linked.

The name GEDCOM is an abbreviation of **GE**nealogical **D**ata **COM**munication. The standard was initiated by the Family History Department of the Church of Jesus Christ of Latter Day Saints (the LDS Church).

What you can do using GEDCOM

- Copy all or part of your family records to a different computer, or another genealogy package
- Take information from other computers, add it to your own records
- Split your genealogy database when it gets too big
- Back up your family records as a GEDCOM file; this copy is available for use in future, even if your computer and package are no longer available.
- Change formats within your genealogy package, or upgrade to a new version
- Add information from the LDS International Genealogical Index (IGI), Ancestral File and Vital Records Index to your family records
- Send your information to be added to the LDS Ancestral File; this is a good way to secure it for the future, whether or not you are in the LDS church
- For members of the LDS Church, submit family information for ordinance work

FamilySearch and Vital Records Index

FamilySearch is a system which provides users at LDS Church Family History Centres and other libraries with extracts from the IGI and Ancestral File, on floppy disk. These extracts can be in GEDCOM format, for transfer into your own genealogy package at home. The LDS Church is publishing Vital Records Indexes for various countries on CDROM for public sale. You can copy records from these in GEDCOM format on your own computer.

Why GEDCOM is needed

- Different genealogy packages have different formats for their databases.
- Many genealogy databases contain characters which might be taken as control characters when transferred from one computer to another. They are particularly likely to give trouble when transferred over communications links.

The intermediate GEDCOM file is different from the structure of any genealogy database. It is an ASCII file avoiding control characters.

GEDCOM is successful

- It is a workable standard.
- It has been amended in areas where it needed improvement.
- It was developed by the LDS church, and is used for transfers to and from their major genealogy databases including Ancestral File and the IGI. It is incorporated into Personal Ancestral File, the genealogy package published by the LDS church.
- It is available for almost all other genealogy packages.
- Information about sources can be transferred from one package to another, using version 5.5 of GEDCOM.

The advantages in having GEDCOM available are such that many people will not consider using a genealogy package without it. With GEDCOM, you can move your family history information to different computers and different packages. The most important result of this is that it makes your data future proof. It can be moved to a different computer when in due course your present one is superseded.

You do not need to know what the GEDCOM format is to use it. The order of information does not matter. If a package encounters information it cannot store, it usually reports it but does not stop storing other information.

Versions of GEDCOM

Versions 1 and 2 of GEDCOM were only used by a few software developers. They are described in Chapter 8, but they are different from later versions, and you are unlikely to encounter them. Versions 3 and 4 of GEDCOM are very similar, and have been used widely. The standard was very general and implementations by different software suppliers varied considerably. The implementation in Personal Ancestral File (PAF) (published by the LDS Church) became the effective transfer standard. After several drafts (versions 5.0 to 5.4), GEDCOM version 5.5 has now become an effectively agreed transfer standard. It extends the definitions from family linkage to source linkage, but it is not such a general standard as versions 3 & 4. Implementations of GEDCOM version 5.5 are closer to each other, and give successful transfer of a wider variety of information than versions 3 & 4.

Personal Ancestral File implementation as Transfer Standard

Chapter 3 of this book describes the PAF implementation of version 3 of GEDCOM in detail. As well as being the effective standard for transfer between different genealogy packages at version 3/4, the family linkage definition and basic structure has remained unchanged for version 5.5. The version 4 GEDCOM standards documents issued by the LDS church included a specification of the Personal Ancestral File implementation (Refs 1,2).

Problems

Although it is successful for transferring basic information and sources, there are sometimes problems in using GEDCOM. The standard is general, and covers a diversity of genealogical information. The standard is not as precise as it should be in some areas. Even different parts of the LDS Church use GEDCOM in different ways, although they initiated the standard. It works well in most applications, transferring names, family relationships, dates, places and sources of vital events; but there are too many quirks and oddities for comfort. This book describes the features of GEDCOM from a practical point of view. It is intended to help you understand any oddities, and point the way to avoiding them.

2. USING GEDCOM

2.1 GEDCOM Transfers: Export and Import

Copying part or all of the family information held in your genealogy package to a GEDCOM file is called **export**. Conversely, you can **import** information from a GEDCOM file to add it into your genealogy package.

GEDCOM import and export are built into the genealogy package. You do not have to buy an extra program called "GEDCOM" - it is already part of the genealogy package. The "import" may be part of a menu called "open a family file" or something similar, with a list of file types, one being "GEDCOM". The "export" might be part of the back-up and file copy facilities of the genealogy package. Just search for "GEDCOM" in the online help system of your genealogy package.

In most packages you can choose the name, disk drive and directory for the GEDCOM file. For example, you can export onto a floppy disk, then move that floppy with its GEDCOM file to another computer. You can also move the information by transferring the GEDCOM file using a communications link.

GEDCOM import is additive. The people from the GEDCOM file are added to the people already in the genealogy database. I recommend that you make your first GEDCOM import into a new empty database. Once you have imported the GEDCOM file into your genealogy package you can browse through the information, and decide which people to add to your existing database. Then you can make a GEDCOM transfer of the selected people from your new database to your main one.

Back up before using GEDCOM

Make sure you have a back up copy of your family records before you use GEDCOM. If adding records to a existing database, you could end with scrambled data if the GEDCOM import is not completed. For these and other transfers, the back up guards against mistakes or mishaps.

GEDCOM Files

A family database in a genealogy package may have several files. For example, one file of individuals, one of notes, one of marriages. Different packages have different ways of organising files; there may be a file of names, or a file of sources. Whatever the organisation in the package, the information is exported into one GEDCOM file.

The one GEDCOM file has numbered records for individuals, and numbered records for families; these numbers are cross-reference identifiers used temporarily by GEDCOM, quite independent of any numbering system in the package. The record for an individual contains references to the families in which the person is a parent or child. The record for a family contains references to the individuals who are parents or children in the family.

The name of a GEDCOM file starts with a part you choose, typically a surname. On MSDOS and similar systems it normally ends with the extension .GED: for example, a file named HAWGOOD.GED for a file with information about my Hawgood family. If a file is too big to fit on one floppy disk it can be split after any complete line. The part on the first disk has the extension .GED, the part on the second disk has extension .G00, on a third disk .G01, etc. On an Apple Macintosh there are no extensions; a set of files on three disks would be SMITH, SMITH(00) and SMITH(01).

Splitting, merging and backing up with GEDCOM

On many packages the recommended way of splitting databases is to use a GEDCOM transfer. Typically you choose one person, then export only the descendants or only the ancestors and their collaterals. To merge databases, you make a GEDCOM import of one into the other, and make linkages to join the two parts. You may have to delete one record of a person who now appears in duplicate; transfer all available information into one record first. In a typical example you decide that a person baptised in one database is the same as a person married in the other database.

A GEDCOM file is a good back up of your family records. Make a copy on a floppy disk (or other removable disk); even if your computer and your genealogy package are destroyed, you will be able to read the GEDCOM file into another genealogy package. This should reconstruct the information and family linkages. The GEDCOM file also has the advantage that all the information and linkages are held as text. Anyone who is familiar with the detail of GEDCOM can read the information, which is the essential first step in reconstructing the information if anything does go awry.

2.2 Versions of GEDCOM

You may need to know about versions of the standard; they are often referred to by the version number of Personal Ancestral File which implemented them. The standards are published by the LDS Church (Refs 1,2,3,6,7). They are quite general, but versions of the standard have been accompanied by a particular GEDCOM implementation in Personal Ancestral File.

GEDCOM version	Personal Ancestral File version
1	(none)
2	2.0
3 (dated Oct 1987)	2.1
4 (dated Aug 1989)	2.2 and 2.3
5.5 (dated Dec 1995)	3.0

GEDCOM version 1 was not used for transfers between packages. There are significant differences between versions 2 and 3, particularly in the areas of date format and family structure. The differences between versions 3 and 4 are in areas like specification of character sets, and specification of calendars. For most GEDCOM files, using version 4 instead of version 3 would not give any changes. For version 4, the standard document was rewritten to be more precise. GEDCOM version 5.5 adds a structure for source references; GEDCOM version 4 is a sub-set of version 5. Versions 5.0 to 5.4 were issued in draft, and implemented by some software developers, but some parts were then removed before version 5.5 was formally issued.

You may have a choice of an implementation for transfer to other packages, or an extended implementation for use in back up, splitting and merging databases, and other operations within one package. The extended implementation may use parts of the GEDCOM standard which are not used by Personal Ancestral File.

2.3 Information available for transfer between packages

If the sender and receiver of information both use the same genealogy package, you should be able to transfer all the information available. You may have to ensure that any optional fields and settings are the same at both ends. If different packages are used, information transferred will either be that in fields common to both packages, or that corresponding to the Personal Ancestral File transfer standard. In a GEDCOM file each individual item of information is accompanied by a tag giving the type of information. This is the feature which enables different packages to make sense of each other's GEDCOM files.

As PAF GEDCOM data was the effective transfer standard, packages try to move in all information which can be held by PAF, even if fields do not correspond. For example, Family History System had no fields for burial date and burial place, but moved the information to a note like "BUR: 21 Jun 1873 Daventry".

Information held by Personal Ancestral File (PAF)

The items of data given below should transfer into any package, as they are the items held by Personal Ancestral File:

Forenames (given names), surname, title, sex.
Date and place of birth, christening, death, burial.
Links to parents and spouses.
Date and place of marriages; whether divorced.
A reference number, independent of the record identity number (RIN) in a particular database.
LDS Ordinances.
Notes about individuals.

Individual, Family and Source

A GEDCOM file from PAF 2.2 has records for individuals and families, with links between them. Source information is held as notes within individual records. PAF 2.2 has no provision for notes within family records, so source information about a marriage has to be held as a note about one of the individuals being married.

PAF 3.0 and most current packages put sources in separate records, following the GEDCOM 5.5 standard. These have cross-reference links to and from individuals or families, organised to show a source for each event. This gives more precise source information, and less duplication. This information can generally be transferred from one package to another.

2.4 Names, Dates, Places and Notes

GEDCOM has special formats for names, dates and places. In addition, Personal Ancestral File has conventions about the entry of notes. These may affect the content of data fields after transfer. There is more about these in Chapter 6, particularly about the format in the GEDCOM file. What follows describes the effects as seen after a transfer.

Dates

Dates in GEDCOM are in the format "23 May 1837", optionally preceded by ABT BEF or AFT for about, before or after. The day or month can be omitted. Many packages have a variety of orders for input and output of dates; you choose the order of day, month and year as an option. You may find that dates disappear unless you change the order temporarily to "day number, month letters, year number" before doing a GEDCOM transfer; look at the manual for your package. Some packages allow entry of free format dates like "Christmas 1837"; these may not appear in full in the receiving package.

Names

Names sometimes get truncated, or moved to notes, or appear with unexpected underscore characters between words. The truncation and moving to notes arise from the different length limits of the packages. For example, PAF 2.2 stores a maximum of three forenames; these and the surname each have a maximum of sixteen characters. (PAF 3.0 removes this restriction on length of names).

Underlining sometimes appears between names. This arises from multi-word forenames or surnames, for example "Jean Marie" and "de la Rue". PAF 2.2 links the words with underscore characters during GEDCOM export, giving "de_la_Rue" and "Jean_Marie". Some packages leave these underscore characters in place during GEDCOM import.

If accents or special symbols seem wrong, you may be able to correct it by choosing a different character set; see page 33.

Places

Places suffer the same truncation as names. For example, PAF 2.1 stores a place as four place names with a maximum of 16 characters each. On GEDCOM export, commas are placed between the place names, for example "Daventry,Northants,England". The slightly odd appearance of place names when transferred to other packages arises from these commas. First, there is no space after the comma in the GEDCOM file, and may not be after import. Second, commas are inserted after "missing" place names. If PAF has "Australia" in the fourth place name field, and nothing in the first, second or third fields, the result is ",,,Australia" in the GEDCOM file, and sometimes in the receiving package. Some packages demand state or country abbreviations as part of the place name; these may appear with commas when transferred to other packages, for example "Los Gatos,,CA".

Notes

Some notes from Personal Ancestral File start with an exclamation mark, for example "!WILL: at Somerset House, proved Feb 1901, all to son John". These are family group notes, generally containing information about sources. In Personal Ancestral File there is an option to print only the notes starting with "!" - but the "!" itself is not printed. On transfer to another package, the exclamation mark may get printed before the text of the note; see page 31.

2.5 Exceptions and errors

During GEDCOM import some packages display a message on the screen if they encounter GEDCOM lines and cannot place the information in the database. Others generate a list of exceptions as a disk file; make sure you look at it after the transfer. Some packages move extra information into notes; for example this is a configuration option in PAF 3.0.

2.6 Modifying GEDCOM files

You can often get round problems by editing the GEDCOM file in a word processor. Make sure the word processor does not add control characters to the file. Use for example "Text Document" in Windows 95/98 WordPad, "Text Only" in Microsoft Word, "DOS text file" in WordPerfect, "ASCII file" in some other word processor packages. But do be careful when viewing or editing a GEDCOM file. Lance Jacobs has warned against making any changes to Ancestral File submissions (Ref 5) because the Ancestral File Operations Unit of the LDS Church has received GEDCOM files corrupted by word processor control characters.

Information to help you modify GEDCOM files is in Chapters 3 to 7. Chapter 3 describes the format of the GEDCOM file, gives a full example from PAF 2.1, and describes the family structure. Chapter 4 gives examples of the way sources are included in GEDCOM 5.5. Chapter 5 lists the tags available for extra information. Chapter 6 gives more detail on the format of names, dates, places and notes. Chapter 7 gives a complete list of tags which are in the GEDCOM 5.5 standard.

3. FEATURES OF GEDCOM VERSIONS 3 & 4, PAF 2.2

This Chapter describes the general structure of GEDCOM, and the structure for family linkages. Examples are from Personal Ancestral File (PAF) version 2.2, using GEDCOM version 4. The PAF 2.1 to 2.3 implementation was the effective transfer standard for GEDCOM versions 3 and 4, and is still used as the most general implementation. GEDCOM version 5.5 is now used by most genealogy packages, including PAF version 3.0; it uses the same family structure but adds a source documentation structure, described in Chapter 4.

GEDCOM data is independent of the data format of any particular package. What follows is a GEDCOM record for one individual, spaced out to distinguish the components.

```
Level  Cross-Reference  Tag   Value
0      @I28@            INDI
1                       NAME  William Henry /Doe/
1                       SEX   M
1                       BIRT
2                       DATE  BEF May 1840
2                       PLAC  Daventry,Northants
1                       FAMS  @F7@ <---- pointer to family record
```

This shows William Henry Doe born before May 1840 at Daventry, Northants. The record for William Henry Doe is numbered, I28; the last line in the example is a pointer to the family, number F7, in which he is a spouse. These numbers are temporary, for use by GEDCOM in holding family relationships, and are enclosed within @ characters. This example uses version 4 of GEDCOM, and is in the format exported by Personal Ancestral File version 2.2.

Each piece of information (**value**) is on a separate **line**. The information is preceded by a **tag** identifying its type, e.g. BIRT for birth and PLAC for place. Tags from PAF 2.2 have three or four letters. The line starts with a **level number** which shows how the information relates to previous lines. For example "2 PLAC" at level 2 refers back to the previous tag at level 1 which is "1 BIRT", so Daventry is the place of birth. A line with level 0 (zero) starts a new GEDCOM record, e.g an individual (tag INDI) or family (tag FAM). The individual or family number in a line at level 0 is between the level number and tag, and is called the **cross-reference identifier**. Every line ends with a **terminator**, a Carriage Return character or a Carriage Return with a Line Feed; as these are non-printing control characters they are not shown specifically in the examples.

Names, dates and places have special formats. The surname is enclosed within / (slash) characters. Dates have day number, first three letters of month, year number. The components of a place name are separated by commas. There is more about these formats in Chapter 6.

Lines are only included if they convey information, and the information can be any length up to a full line, with continuation on further lines. Thus the GEDCOM format caters for a variable number of variable length fields.

The individual record (I28) for William Henry Doe is above. What follows is the GEDCOM record for the family (F7) in which he is husband:

```
0 @F7@ FAM
1 HUSB @I28@
1 WIFE @I16@
1 CHIL @I17@
1 CHIL @I18@
1 MARR
2 DATE 14 MAY 1863
2 PLAC Sheaf St Indepen,Daventry,Northants
```

The family record mainly consists of pointers to the individuals in the family. Each pointer is double-ended; the individual record has a pointer to the family, the family has a corresponding pointer to the individual. The rest of the file is in section 3.1. From this you can trace the wife I16 as Elizabeth Roe, the first child I17 as John Doe born 1865, the second child I18 as Elizabeth Doe born 1867.

To make sense of a GEDCOM file, first remember that every line starting with a digit 0 is the beginning of a new record; most are individual and family records. In most examples in this book I have added a blank line between records to make it easier to see the structure. For PAF 2.2 the records for individuals in a family must come before the record for that family; otherwise the order of records in the file does not matter. Family structure is held by making individuals point at their families, and families point at their individuals.

If you look at a GEDCOM file you need to appreciate this basic structure to find your way about. If you look at the file with a word processor you can use "search" to find pointers. For example a search for @F7@ in the file in section 3.1 would find all the individuals in that family, then the family record. Note the warning on page 8 about corrupting GEDCOM files with word processor control characters.

3.1 GEDCOM from Personal Ancestral File 2.1 to 2.31

On the next three pages there are edit screens from PAF 2.2 for an individual, notes for that individual, a marriage in which he is the husband, and the complete GEDCOM file exported from PAF 2.2 for this family. If exported from PAF 2.1 the only difference in the file would be the one line in the header record which specifies the source system. The data is fictitious, invented to show features of GEDCOM. The tree below shows this family:

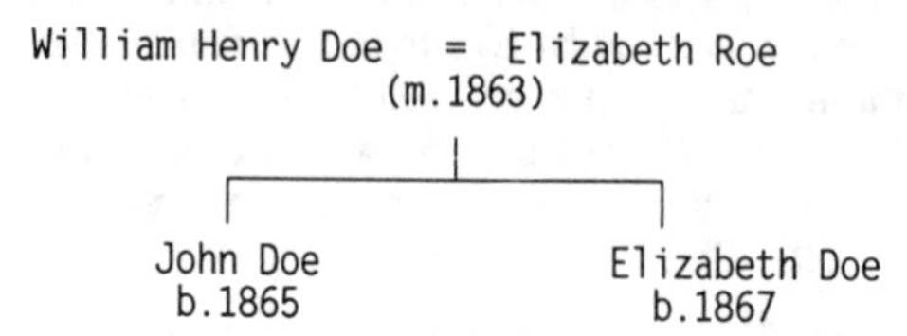

The PAF 2.2 implementation of GEDCOM was the effective standard for GEDCOM version 4 data to be transferred between different genealogy packages. PAF versions 2.1 and 2.2 comply with GEDCOM versions 3 and 4. GEDCOM version 3 or 4 exported from another package may have additional tags, but for the common information it should follow the format of the file given here for successful transfer to any other package.

In Section 3.2 there is a list of tags used in the PAF 2.2 implementation of GEDCOM. The current standard is GEDCOM 5.5. It has a source structure, and many more event and attribute types are generally used and agreed than in GEDCOM 3 & 4. But it has just the same family structure as GEDCOM versions 3 & 4.

GEDCOM File exported from PAF 2.2

The listing on this page and page 13 is a complete GEDCOM file.

```
0 HEAD
1 SOUR PAF 2.2
1 DEST PAF
1 DATE 3 JAN 1991
1 FILE DOE6.GED
```

Header record
First record in file

```
0 @S1@ SUBM
1 NAME David Hawgood
1 ADDR 26 Cloister Road
2 CONT Acton
2 CONT London W3 ODE
1 PHON 081 993 2897
1 COMM Data is fictitious for test purposes.
```

Submitter record

```
0 @I16@ INDI
1 NAME Elizabeth /Roe/
1 SEX F
1 FAMS @F7@
```

Individual record

```
0 @I17@ INDI
1 NAME John /Doe/
1 SEX M
1 BIRT
2 DATE 1865
2 PLAC Coventry
1 BAPL SUBMITTED
1 ENDL SUBMITTED
1 FAMC @F7@
```

Individual record

```
0 @I18@ INDI
1 NAME Elizabeth /Doe/
1 SEX F
1 BIRT
2 DATE 1867
2 PLAC Coventry
1 FAMC @F7@
```

Individual record

(file continues on page 13)

```
                         INDIVIDUAL DATA                  (Edit)
Sex:M    SURNAME:Doe          Given1:William                RIN:28
         Given2:Henry         Given3:              Title:Mr

BIRTH        Date:Bef   May 1840
  PLACE  Level 1:Daventry           Level 2:Northants
         Level 3:                   Level 4:
CHRISTENING Date:25 May 1840
  PLACE      L 1:Sheaf St Indepen      L 2:Daventry
             L 3:Northants             L 4:
DEATH        Date:Abt   Nov 1900
  PLACE      L 1:23 Sheaf St           L 2:Daventry
             L 3:Northants             L 4:England
BURIAL       Date:Aft   Nov 1900
  PLACE      L 1:                      L 2:
             L 3:Northants             L 4:

BAPTISM      Date:25 Apr 1990       Temple Code:LN
ENDOWMENT    Date:See Notes         Temple Code:
SEAL to PAR  Date:Submitted         Temple Code:      ID NO.:A121
```

```
In 1880 Kelly's Directory as carpenter, of Sheaf Street Daventry. In 1881
Census for Sheaf St Daventry as carpenter, age 41, born Daventry.

!WILL: at Somerset House, proved Feb 1901, all to son John

LDS Endowment entries are invented, and may not be in correct format

"Sheaf St Indepen" is abbreviated from "Sheaf Street Independent"
in places of marriage and christening
```

```
                              MARRIAGE DATA
MRIN:7
            Husband Name:William Doe-28
               Wife Name:Elizabeth Roe-16

MARRIAGE              Date:14 May 1863
           PLACE  Level 1:Sheaf St Indepen     Level 2:Daventry
                        Level   3:Northants               Level   4:

SEAL Wife to Husband  Date:26 Apr 1990                Temple  Code:LN
```

Individual, Notes and Marriage Data edit screens from PAF 2.2

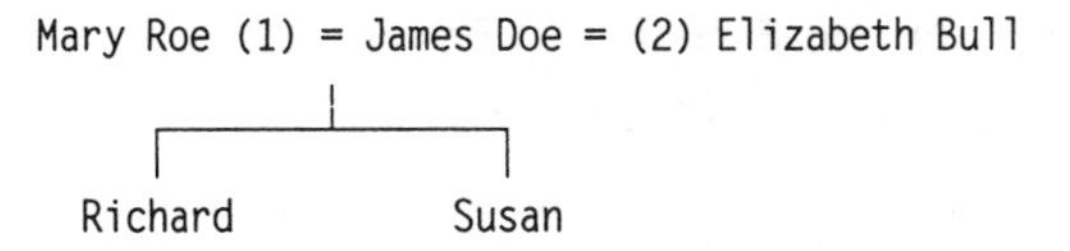

The family tree shows the spouses and children of James Doe. The cross reference pointers only apply within one particular GEDCOM file. They may be quite different from the RINs and MRINs (Record Identity Numbers and Marriage Record Identity Numbers) in the genealogy database from which the GEDCOM file derives (sometimes they are the same, particularly if there have been no deletions from the database).

The order of children within a family is shown by the order of the CHIL lines within the family records; the order of the individual records within the GEDCOM file is not significant. I104 Richard Doe is first child in family F073, I103 Susan Doe is second child. Similarly the order of "FAMS" lines within an individual record shows which family comes first. James Doe's first family is F073, his second family is F082.

Cross-references do not have to start with I for Individual, F for Family, and do not have to be a fixed length; they just have to be unique within a particular GEDCOM file.

3.5 Marriages and Families

The presence of a family record in the GEDCOM file does not necessarily indicate an actual marriage; the children in the family may be illegitimate. There is no specific provision in GEDCOM versions 3 & 4 for indicating that there was a marriage, but the date and place are unknown. GEDCOM 5.5 does have provision for indicating that there is a marriage, although the date and place are unknown - see page 22.

3.6 LDS Ordinances and Submissions

Members of the LDS church use GEDCOM to submit family information for ordinance work. As Personal Ancestral File is published by the LDS church, and GEDCOM was originated by the LDS church, there is special provision for ordinances.

Most users of GEDCOM are not members of the LDS church, and ignore the LDS ordinance fields. However they are almost certain to encounter them if using files downloaded from the IGI and Ancestral File on CD-ROM. For this reason I have included LDS ordinances and their GEDCOM tags in the examples. I have not attempted to include comprehensive information about them.

3.7 Sources in GEDCOM versions 3 & 4

In GEDCOM 3 & 4 there was no agreed way of transferring source information between systems except as notes about individuals. The GEDCOM standards provides for holding source information in such a way that it is not duplicated. Version 3 of the GEDCOM standard encouraged the use of a source record (at level 0) with information about several individuals, but this was never implemented in PAF 2.2. Version 4 of the GEDCOM standard did not describe the use of source records, although the tags were still available. With general implementation of GEDCOM version 5.5 source references have become standard and transferable, as described in Chapter 4. Several packages, for example Roots III and Pedigree, implemented source structures in GEDCOM 3 & 4. The methods are similar to those in GEDCOM 5.5, but different in detail. There are some notes on this in page 20.

3.8 Header, Trailer, Submitter and Submission Records

These records contain information about the GEDCOM file, housekeeping information.

The trailer is a single line at the end of the file, either "0 TRLR" or "0 EOF". PAF exports TRLR but recognises either TRLR or EOF as ending the file on import.

The header at the start of the file has source system, destination system, date, filename and character set information. The first line is "0 HEAD". There is an example in section 3.1. Source and destination are genealogy package names or abbreviations for them.

The submitter record follows the header; it contains name, address, and phone number of the submitter, and comments. PAF export makes this line "0 @S1@ SUBM". The cross-reference pointer is there for compatibility with future systems having information from several submitters in one file.

PAF 2.2 only exports a submission record if the GEDCOM file is a submission to Ancestral File, or a submission from an LDS church member for LDS ordinances. The record starts with the line "0 SUBN". An example from a file exported from PAF 2.2 for submission to Ancestral File just had:

```
0 SUBN
1 TYPE Descendant
1 INDI @I6-1@
```

The submission was for descendants of the person who appeared in the GEDCOM file with cross-reference @I6-1@.

The LDS Church vet genealogy packages to authorise them for Ancestral File submissions, so this type of GEDCOM file should not be changed between exporting it from the package and sending it to the LDS. See Refs 4, 5.

3.9 Spaces between components of a GEDCOM line

The GEDCOM standards from version 3 on say there must be a space after the level number, and there must be a space before the tag. Earlier versions of the standard did not demand these spaces, and some implementations which are nominally at version 3/4 do not put the spaces in. PAF 2.2 accepts GEDCOM without these spaces; for example it treats "0 @23@INDI" (no space between @ and INDI) as being the same as "0 @23@ INDI" (one space between @ and INDI).

4. SOURCES IN GEDCOM VERSION 5.5, PAF 3.0

This Chapter describes the way source records and references are held in GEDCOM 5.5, the current standard, used by many genealogy packages including Personal Ancestral File version 3.0.

4.1 Source, citation, repository and call number

As well as the family structure of individual and family records, there is a structure of source and repository records. Each event or other fact can have a pointer to a source document record. Each source document can have a pointer to the record for the repository at which it can be consulted. The event has a citation, for example a page number, within the source document. The source document has a call number within the repository.

The example is part of a GEDCOM file exported from Personal Ancestral File 3.0. It shows the 1871 census being used as source for information about birth of my ancestor William Lilburn, a police detective inspector.

```
0 @I11@ INDI                                                    Individual record
1 NAME William /Lilburn/
1 SEX M
1 BIRT
2 DATE 1815
2 PLAC Lincoln,England
2 SOUR @S6@                                          Cross-reference to source ⇒ ┐
3 PAGE folio 69, 11 Croft St.            Source citation within that source   │
3 DATA                                                                        │
4 TEXT head, mar, age 55, Police Inspector, b. Lincoln                        │
0 @S6@ SOUR                                                   Source record ⇐ ┘
1 AUTH Registrar General
1 TITL 1871 census St. Swithin, Lincoln
1 PUBL on microfilm by Public Record Office
1 REPO @R1@                                      Cross-reference to repository ⇒ ┐
2 CALN RG10/3372                      Call number for source at that repository   │
0 @R1@ REPO                                               Repository record ⇐ ┘
1 NAME Family Records Centre
1 ADDR Myddelton Street
2 CONT London EC1R 1UW
1 PHON 0181 876 3444
```

Cross-reference to source
The individual record has the BIRT tag for birth at level 1 followed by the DATE and PLAC (place) at level 2. These are followed by a SOUR tag with cross-reference pointer @S@6. The SOUR tag is at level 2, showing it refers to the BIRT at level 1.

Citation within that source
Following the source tag in the individual record is the information about the particular entry in the source document. The PAGE tag - at level 3 to show it refers to the source at level 2 - shows that the location within the document is "folio 69, 11 Croft St". This is followed by a DATA tag also at level 3, and a TEXT tag at level 4 with the actual entry from the census.

Source record
To see what source @S6@ refers to, look down the file for the source record starting 0 @S6@ SOUR. This shows that the author is the Registrar General, the title is the 1871 census for St. Swithin, Lincoln, and that it has been published on microfilm by the Public Record Office.

Cross-reference to repository
This information is followed by a cross-reference pointer to repository @R1@, with tag REPO.

Call number for source at that repository
At level 2 to show it refers to the repository is the tag CALN with the call number RG10/3372.

Repository record
Finally in this example there is the record for the repository, starting 0 @R1@ REPO. This has the repository name, its address (with a continuation line shown by tag CONT), and its phone number.

Clearly there can be many documents in one repository, and one document can be the source for information about many different people in the particular family. Note that GEDCOM 5.5 does not provide for the repository record having pointers to the records for the source documents consulted there, nor for the source record to have pointers to the individuals (or families) for which it is the source.

4.2 Quality of Data

Some packages have provision for a "Quality of data" or "Certainty Assessment" against information. This is built in to the GEDCOM standard 5.5. The quality is expressed as a digit from 0 to 3, with meanings:

0	Unreliable evidence or estimated data
1	Questionable reliability of evidence (interviews, census, oral genealogies, or potential for bias, for example an autobiography)
2	Secondary evidence, data officially recorded sometime after event
3	Direct and primary evidence used, or by dominance of the evidence

This appears with a tag QUAY subsidiary to the source reference, for example adding it to the example above to show the census as "direct and primary evidence" would give:

```
2 SOUR @S6@
3 PAGE folio 69, 11 Croft St.
3 QUAY 3
```

4.3 Other implementations of source structures

For systems without source records, the GEDCOM 5.5 standard allows the SOUR tag to be followed by a value (and continuation lines) instead of a pointer.

```
1 BIRT
2 DATE 1815
2 PLAC Lincoln,England
2 SOUR 1871 census St. Swithin, Lincoln;
3 CONT Call number RG10/3372 at Family Records Centre
```

Packages which implemented source structures in GEDCOM 3 & 4 were all different. In Pedigree the source record has pointers to individuals, individual records have pointers to sources. In Roots III, the source cross-reference is the same as that in GEDCOM 5.5, but the source record is different, having a value on the same line as the tag at level 0:

```
1 DEAT
2 DATE 14 APR 1905
2 PLAC Stamford, Fairfield, CT
2 SOUR @S5@
0 @S5@ SOUR City of Stamford Records, Death Certificate 12588
```

As well as source records, Roots III had "Title" records to cross-reference documents by title.

5. EVENTS AND ATTRIBUTES IN GEDCOM 5.5

Standard and non-standard events and attributes

Over 600 tags were specified in the GEDCOM standard version 4. Version 5.5 specifies a much smaller selection of tags, about 130, as being in the Lineage-linked tag definition. (These are listed in Chapter 7). The events and attributes for which there are standard tags in GEDCOM 5.5 are described in sections 5.1 to 5.7. Ways of including other events and attributes are described in sections 5.8 and 5.9. Packages vary widely in which events to include. PAF 3.0 has the same events as PAF 2.1: birth, christening, marriage, divorce, burial, death, plus LDS ordinances. Ultimate Family Tree, The Master Genealogist, Family Origins, Family Tree Maker and others have a wide selection of events and attributes.

5.1 Individual events - standard tags

The following are given in the GEDCOM standard version 5.5 as the tags which can appear as individual events:

```
ADOP  Adoption; can be followed by a link to the adopting family, see page 32
BAPL  LDS Baptism
BAPM  Baptism
BARM  Bar Mitzvah
BASM  Bas Mitzvah
BIRT  Birth
BLES  Blessing
BURI  Burial or other disposal of mortal remains of a person
CENS  Census
CHR   Christening
CHRA  Adult Christening
CONF  Confirmation
CONL  LDS Confirmation
CREM  Cremation
DEAT  Death
EMIG  Emigration
ENDL  LDS Endowment
EVEN  Event - should be qualified by TYPE, see 5.8 page 24
FCOM  First Communion
GRAD  Graduation
IMMI  Immigration
NATU  Naturalisation
ORDN  Ordination
PROB  Probate
RETI  Retirement
SLGC  LDS Sealing to Child
WILL  Will (date should be that of signing -there is a PROB tag for probate)
```

For these individual events, and for the family events in the next section, the standard says that the only value allowed on the same line as the tag is the letter Y to show an event occurred but no details are available. Examples of the allowed formats are:

```
1 RETI
2 DATE 1877
2 PLAC Lincoln
2 NOTE Police Detective Inspector

1 DEAT Y                (shows death has occurred, but no details are known)
```

5.2 Family Events - standard tags

The following are given in the GEDCOM standard version 5.5 as the tags which can appear as family events:

```
ANUL  Annulment
CENS  Census
DIV   Divorce
DIVF  Filing for Divorce
ENGA  Engagement
EVEN  Event - should be qualified by TYPE
SLGS  LDS Sealing to Spouse
MARR  Marriage - legal, common law or customary to form a family unit
MARB  Banns of Marriage
MARC  Marriage contract
MARL  Marriage licence
MARS  Marriage settlement
```

The format for these family events is the same as that for individual events, as given in the previous section. Thus the only value on the same line as one of these tags should be "Y" to show the event occurred. The GEDCOM line to show a marriage occurred but no details are available would be:

```
1 MARR Y
```

5.3 Individual Attributes

The following are given in the GEDCOM standard 5.5 as being allowable tags for individual attributes.

```
CAST  Caste
DSCR  Physical Description
EDUC  Education
IDNO  Identity Number - should be qualified to show which nation or organisation
NATI  Nationality
NCHI  Number of children
NMR   Number of marriages
OCCU  Occupation
PROP  Property
RELI  Religion
RESI  Residence
SSN   US Social Security Number
TITL  Title
```

Note that these attribute tags can have a value on the same line as the tag, and that date, place, source etc are subsidiary, for example:

```
1 OCCU licensed victualler
2 DATE 1854
2 PLAC Portsea, Hampshire
```

5.4 LDS Ordinances

Tags for LDS Ordinances in GEDCOM 5.5 are included in the list in Chapter 7.

Examples of the way LDS ordinances appear in GEDCOM from PAF 2.1 are given in section 3.1. There are some changes in the way they appear in GEDCOM 5.5; see the GEDCOM standard for details.

5.5 Detail for events and attributes

Events and attributes differ in that there can be a value on the same line as an attribute tag, but there cannot be a value (except a letter Y to show the event happened) on the same line as an event tag. As the distinction is rather arbitrary, this is one area in which packages are quite likely to depart from the present standard.

Apart from this, events and attributes can all have the same selection of additional information. There are full details of the allowed formats in the GEDCOM 5.5 standard. There can be a TYPE, DATE, place structure, address structure, AGE at event, responsible agency (AGNC), cause of event (CAUS), source citation, note structure, and multimedia link.

5.6 Other tags for individuals

SEX Sex, M or F

Tags followed by cross-reference pointers to individuals and submitters

SUBM Submitter; points at the submitter record for the person providing information about this individual. The person referenced as submitter in the header record is taken as applying to the whole file, unless there are specific references in individual records.

ALIA Alias; points at an individual record for someone who may be the same person, who may have the same name or a different name, see page 27

ANCI Ancestor interest; points at a submitter record, showing interest in research on ancestors of this individual.

DESI Descendant interest; pointing to a submitter record, showing interest in research on descendants of this individual.

ASSO Association; points at individual record for an associated individual, eg godfather, executor, witness, or points at a submitter record to show how the submitter is related to the individual; followed by TYPE and RELA tags, see page 32.

5.7 Tags followed by reference numbers

REFN Reference number allocated by user; followed by a TYPE tag to show the numbering system, eg page and position number within a set of pedigree charts, or ancestor number on Ahnentafel/Sosa Stradonitz system, or user's own system.

RFN Record File Number, permanent number within a particular computer file

AFN Ancestral File Number, number allocated by the LDS Church Family History Department on receipt of an Ancestral File Submission; use it to show that someone in a later submission is the same person.

RIN Record Identity Number, allocated automatically by computer, and may change when files are reorganised, merged or split.

5.8 Information with no standard tag

Draft and issued versions of GEDCOM standards have given several different ways of transferring information about events, attributes and other information not in the standard list of tags. Software developers have adopted these from the draft standards, only to find that the later formally issued standard is different. Unfortunately the effect of this is that the implementations in some software packages do not conform to GEDCOM standard version 5.5, but do conform to some earlier draft such as 5.0 or 5.3.

There are three ways given in the 5.5 standard for transferring extra events and attributes: notes, EVEN tags, and non-standard tags starting with an underscore. Notes are the most general, and can be imported without trouble to any other package. EVEN and tags with underscore are likely to be understood only by other versions of the issuing package.

5.8.1 Note

The example for the note, and for the other methods, is the apprenticeship of Elizabeth Excell.

```
1 NOTE Apprenticed in 1733 to Mary Blakely of St Clement Danes, mantua maker
```

Notes can continue over many lines or be in separate records - see page 31.

One package which uses notes a great deal is Personal Ancestral File. It has very few set fields - the only events are birth, christening, marriage, divorce, death and burial, plus LDS ordinances. All other events are put in general notes.

5.8.2 EVEN tag

The second way is to use an EVEN tag. The format for showing events and attributes not in the list with the EVEN tag is:

```
1 EVEN
2 TYPE Apprenticed
2 DATE 1733
2 PLAC St Clement Danes
2 NOTE Master is Mary Blakely, mantua maker
```

My reading of the GEDCOM standard is that there should not be a value on the same line as the tag EVEN. But the standard says it can be used for events or attributes -and attribute tags can have a value on the same line. The package Family Origins puts a value on the same line if EVEN is being used for an attribute, for example:

```
1 EVEN D. Phil (Heidelberg)
2 TYPE Degree
```

5.8.3 Non-standard tag with underscore

The third way is to use a non-standard tag, which must start with an underscore. This can then be used consistently throughout files generated by a software package, for example a tag for apprenticeship might be _APPR, and the format would be:

```
1 _APPR
2 DATE 1733
2 PLAC St Clement Danes
2 NOTE Master is Mary Blakely, mantua maker
```

Non-standard tags with underscore are used extensively by Family Tree Maker, particularly for marital status.

5.9 SCHEMA to define non-standard tags

If you come across tags SCHEMA or _SCHEMA in a GEDCOM file, what follows may help you understand the file. Otherwise skip this section - SCHEMA is not in the GEDCOM 5.5 standard.

Earlier drafts of GEDCOM version 5 included provision for a SCHEMA, which is a set of data item definitions, and their descriptions. In GEDCOM this also defined their non-standard tags. It turned out to be complex to implement, so it is not included in version 5.5 of the GEDCOM standard. But some software developers implemented it. The format is to have a tag SCHEMA in the header, followed by the record types, and definitions of tags for each. This would appear as:

```
1 SCHEMA
2 INDI
3 _APPR
4 LABL Apprenticed
```

The tag _APPR would then be used as required in individual records.

As SCHEMA is not a valid tag in GEDCOM 5.5, some packages have replaced it by _SCHEMA, but kept the structure following it, to show how non-standard tags are used. For example Family Tree Maker at versions up to 4.4 had 13 facts which could be allocated meanings by the user. They appear in GEDCOM output with a tag _SCHEMA in the header, followed by definitions of the 13 facts as tags _FA1 to _FA13. If the user had allocated Fact 1 as "Apprenticed" part of the header in GEDCOM export would be:

```
1 _SCHEMA
2 INDI
3 _FA1
4 Apprenticed
```

6. SPECIAL TYPES OF INFORMATION: PLACE, NAME, DATE etc

6.1 Places

Identification of a place may require several different place names, for example a parish, a town, a county and a country. In GEDCOM the names progress from the smallest unit to the largest, and are separated by commas. The following examples are places as they appear in a GEDCOM file from the IGI:

```
Saint John The Baptist, Shoreditch, London, England
Bideford, Devon, England
```

On export from PAF there is no space after the commas between the levels of the place name. For example:

```
Sunninghill,Berkshire,England
```

In PAF 2.2, a place can have up to 4 levels. If a level is blank, the GEDCOM value can have a leading comma, or adjacent commas:

```
Kensington,London,,England (third level blank)
,Coventry,Warwickshire,England (first level blank)
,Coventry (first, third and fourth levels blank)
```

The manual for PAF 2.2 encourages use of the four levels in a consistent way, for example making the third level always the county, and the fourth level always the country. Different packages divide place names in quite different ways, so you tend to get odd-looking place names when you export from one package and import into another. For example, the IGI and Ancestral File do not insert an additional comma if a level is blank; the country is always last, but may be third or fourth.

In GEDCOM 5.5 there is a way of specifying the usage of the levels if they are to be used in a consistent way. In the header record, there can be a structure with place and format, for example:

```
1 PLAC
2 FORM parish, town, county, country
```

There is then provision for over-riding the format for the place within a particular event. The standard discourages use of this.

In some packages lengths of place names are limited. The most extreme was PAF 2.2, where the four parts of a place names were limited to 16 characters each. During import, a name over 16 characters was truncated, and this was reported in the exception listing. PAF 3.0 has removed the restriction, but similar effects may be encountered on other packages.

6.2 Names

6.2.1 Name format

In GEDCOM 3 & 4 the full name is on one line; the surname is enclosed in slash characters. In GEDCOM 5.5 an individual's name must appear first in the same way:

```
1 NAME Alexandre /Delorme/       (surname Delorme)
1 NAME Alexandre /De Lorme/ (surname De Lorme)
1 NAME Alexandre De /Lorme/ (surname Lorme)
```

The GEDCOM standard allows for the name to continue after the surname, e.g:

```
1 NAME John /Doe/ the third
```

In GEDCOM 5.5 components of the name can follow at level 2:

```
NPFX  Prefix, eg Dr
GIVN  Given names
NICK  Nickname
SPFX  Surname Prefix
SURN  Surname
NSFX  Suffix
```

TITL (Title) is not part of this name structure, it is a separate attribute.

Notes and sources can follow names - or almost any part of the GEDCOM structure. Examples:

```
1 NAME Rev. Joseph Henry /Bowker/
2 GIVN Joseph Henry
2 SURN Bowker
2 NICK Joe
2 NPFX Rev.
2 NOTE Known in the Robinson family as "Uncle Joe"
2 SOUR @S23@
1 NAME Alexandre De /Lorme/
2 GIVN Alexandre
2 SURN Lorme
2 SPFX De
```

I believe that at present most packages import the surname value after the NAME tag and ignore the SURN value.

6.2.2 Names in PAF 2.1 to 2.3

There are some features of names in GEDCOM from PAF 2.1 to 2.3 which do not generally occur in other packages, and do not occur in PAF 3.0. One is that if a forename or a surname contains spaces, they are replaced by underscore characters. In the following example one forename is "Jean Marie", the surname is "de la Rue":

```
NAME Jean_Marie Phillippe /de_la_Rue/
```

PAF 2.2 can only hold 16 characters for the surname, and 16 for each of three forenames. On import, PAF 2.2 truncates any part of a name which is over 16 characters.

Extra space characters for "missing" forenames

On export PAF 2.2 puts one space in the GEDCOM file between forenames, and also puts an extra space for any forename field which is blank.

```
John William Henry/Doe/
John William /Doe - one space after William because 3rd forename is blank.
John  /Doe/ - two spaces after John because 2nd and 3rd forenames are blank
```

Most packages ignore the extra spaces, and the GEDCOM standard says spaces should not be significant, but at least one package, Family Tree Print, expected the "correct" number of spaces for missing forenames.

6.2.3 Alternative name, Alias

There does not seem to be a generally accepted way of giving alternative names, there are several methods. The GEDCOM 5.5 standard says that if a person has an alternative name, the individual record should have a tag ALIA with a cross-reference to a record with that name. An example would be:

```
0 @1@ INDI
1 NAME Charles John /Leder/
1 ALIA @2@
0 @2@ INDI
1 NAME Karl Johann /Leder/
```

It also says the NAME tag can appear several times in the individual record:

```
0 @1@ INDI
1 NAME Charles John /Leder/
1 NAME Karl Johann /Leder/
```

The standard says the first should be the preferred name, but admits that some packages, in particular PAF, only keep the last one encountered in the GEDCOM record. In practice most genealogy packages consider the alternative name as an attribute. For example Family Tree Maker uses the format:

```
0 @1@ INDI
1 NAME Charles John /Leder/
1 ALIA Karl Johann /Leder/
```

The manual for PAF 3.0 says it is permissible to put "or" in a name. This would appear as:

```
1 NAME Charles John or Karl Johann /Leder/
```

This is used in GEDCOM from the IGI on CDROM; for example

```
1 NAME William /HAWGOOD OR ALLGOOD/
```

If you enter alternative names in a genealogy package, add a note to say how each was used, for example:

```
2 NOTE Born 1845 in Switzerland as Karl Johann
3 CONT 1878 marriage to 1922 death in England as Charles John
```

6.3 Dates

6.3.1 Date format

Date formats in GEDCOM cater for exact, approximate and calculated dates, periods, ranges, different calendars, and even dates given in words relative to a festival or historical events. Unfortunately the tag DATE can also be followed by words implying that an event did or did not happen (Dead, Not Married), and words implying age at event (Infant). Most dates in GEDCOM files transfer without any problem, but if you encounter one that is reported as an exception during GEDCOM import it is worth looking at the form in the GEDCOM file; the date intended will usually be readily apparent.

In GEDCOM the basic format of a date, following the tag DATE, is the day number in digits, 3-letter abbreviation of the name of the month, then four digits for the year:

```
2 DATE 20 JUL 1837
```

Variations allowed in GEDCOM 3 & 4, still in GEDCOM 5.5, and widely used, are that the day number or month name can be omitted; the date can be preceded by abbreviations ABT about, BEF before, AFT after:

```
ABT 1850
BEF NOV 1920
AFT 3 NOV 1920
```

For an old-style date, eg dates up to 24th March in years up to 1751 in England, the last two digits of the second year follow a slash:

```
19 FEB 1715/16
19 FEB 1699/00
```

See the next section for the use of a slash in date ranges like 1760/1770.

6.3.2 Dates in GEDCOM 5.5

Different packages vary in which parts of the extended definitions of dates allowed in GEDCOM 5.5 are used. What follows is intended to help you interpret dates you find in GEDCOM. Be sure to read the GEDCOM standard if constructing dates in GEDCOM - there are some comments on preferred practice.

Approximation can be shown by:
EST for estimated (eg if a birth date is based on the average age at marriage of 25 for men)
CAL for Calculated (eg if a birth date is taken from age at death).
< > (Angle brackets) around the date - for example:

```
2 DATE <1820>
```

INT for Interpreted is used where a year or full date can be derived from a phrase. The derived part follows INT, then the date phrase follows in brackets:

```
2 DATE INT 1820 (Summer 1820)
2 DATE INT 25 Dec 1851 (Christmas Day 1851)
```

Periods between beginning and ending years or dates are shown by FROM and TO:

```
2 DATE FROM 1742
2 DATE TO 23 Oct 1877
2 DATE FROM 1851 TO 1871
```

Ranges of dates within which an event is estimated to have occurred are shown by BET (between) with AND, for example:

```
1 DEAT
2 DATE BET 1840 AND 1870
3 NOTE Married 1840, deceased at son's marriage 1870
```

It is always worth adding a note to explain the reasoning when giving a range.

In GEDCOM 3 & 4 some packages used the two years separated by a slash to show a period or range of years, a dual date. This use of the slash for a range or period is not included in the GEDCOM standard 5.5, but in practice it is still used by some packages.

```
1760/1770
```

6.3.3 Keywords as date values

In the GEDCOM 5.5 standard dates in LDS ordinances can contain special words like SUBMITTED. The standard says that other dates should not contain keywords, but acknowledges that packages use them, for example Personal Ancestral File (at version 3 as well as 2.1) can show an infant death as:

```
1 DEAT
2 DATE INFANT
```

PAF 3 uses keywords to show a couple were not married:

```
1 MARR
2 DATE NOT MARRIED
```

Family Tree Maker (v5) uses keywords such as UNKNOWN and DEAD to show an event occurred, but date is not known:

```
1 BIRT
2 DATE UNKNOWN
1 DEAT
2 DATE Dead
```

If you receive a GEDCOM file with keywords as dates the meaning is probably clear if you examine the GEDCOM file with a word processor, and in some cases automatic processing will allow for these keywords coming from well-known packages. If generating a GEDCOM file to send away, it is better to edit the individuals and marriages to include an estimated date, and add a note to say this has been done, eg

```
1 BIRT
2 DATE EST 1790
2 NOTE Rough estimate based on daughter being married in 1840
```

6.3.4 Change date of record

In PAF 3, and other packages, the date and time of the last change to each record is stored; this is within the record with a tag CHAN at level 1 followed by DATE and TIME tags.

```
1 CHAN
2 DATE 04 Nov 1998
3 TIME 14:06:26
```

6.3.5 Calendar

Version 4 of the GEDCOM standard introduced a way of specifying a date from a calendar other than a conventional Gregorian one. This facility was removed from drafts of GEDCOM 5, but included again in GEDCOM 5.5 following comments from software developers who used it. Few packages support non-standard dates at present, let alone non-standard calendars. The calendar is shown by an escape sequence @#Dcalendar-name@ before the date value. Note that this appears against each date, not in the header. Allowed values in GEDCOM 5.5 are:

```
@@#DGREGORIAN@ - the default Gregorian calendar
@@#DJULIAN@ - Julian, uses Day Month Year as for Gregorian
@@#DHEBREW@ - uses abbreviations of Hebrew month names, eg Tsh for Tishri
@@#DFRENCH R@ - uses abbreviations of French Revolutionary month names,
                eg Pluv for Pluviose.
```

An example of the format is:

```
2 DATE @#DHEBREW@ 1 Tsh 5561
```

The PAF 2.2 GEDCOM specification says specifically that it does not support calendar escape sequences, and treats anything enclosed within @ signs as a cross-reference pointer. The GEDCOM 4 specification said that there should be no space character between the escape sequence and the date.

6.4 Age at event

Age normally follows an individual event. The standard says numbers should be followed by y for years, m for months, d for days; in practice years are usually given as a number alone. For example:

```
1 CENS
2 DATE 1881
2 AGE 4m
1 DEAT
2 DATE 1915
2 AGE 34
```

For a family event, within a family record, the GEDCOM 5.5 standard provides a way to show which partner the age refers to. For example (the oldest groom in my family records, Fred Lilburn marrying Eva Lawson):

```
1 MARR
2 DATE 25 May 1947
2 PLAC Register Office, Lincoln
2 HUSB
3 AGE 71
2 WIFE
3 AGE 65
```

The age value can include > (greater than) and < (less than) symbols. It can also include keywords:

```
CHILD age less than 8 years
INFANT age less than 1 year
STILLBORN died before or near birth
```

6.5 Notes

There can be a NOTE tag subsidiary to almost any record, event, attribute or other tag. Those commonly used are a note for each individual, each family, each event or attribute.

6.5.1 Continuation and concatenation

A note can extend over many lines, using subsidiary tags CONT for continued and CONC for concatenation. The difference between these is that the value after CONT starts on a new line, the value after CONC continues without a line break. The two GEDCOM lines:

```
1 NOTE He appears as a carpenter in the 1880 Kelly's Directory for Daventry
1 CONC and in the 1881 census for Sheaf St Daventry.
```

join up into one continuous paragraph:

> He appears as a carpenter in the 1880 Kelly's Directory for Daventry and in the 1881 census for Sheaf St Daventry.

The two GEDCOM lines:

```
1 NOTE Pawnbroker in White's Portsmouth directory 1859.
2 CONT Loan & Discount Banker in White's Portsmouth directory 1867.
```

are imported into two separate lines:

> Pawnbroker in White's Portsmouth directory 1859.
> Loan & Discount Banker in White's Portsmouth directory 1867.

6.5.2 Notes in PAF 2.2

PAF 2.2 puts all notes about an individual together, and does not put any notes against a family or marriage. However there can be several different notes about an individual, separated on the PAF notes screen by a blank line, see Figure 3.1.

```
1 NOTE !WILL: at Somerset House, proved Feb 1901, all to son John
```

This example includes two conventions about notes used in PAF. A note starting with an exclamation mark is a "family group note". Only these notes are printed on family group sheets, and included in Ancestral File Submissions. The other convention is the "tagged note". PAF 2.2 encouraged the user to start notes holding source information with standard tag words like !WILL, !BURIAL, !BIRTH, and to start other notes with standard tag words like "OCCUPATION:". This type of standard tag word is within the text of the note, as seen on display screens. It is different from the GEDCOM tag OCCU which only appears within GEDCOM files. There are shareware add-on programs which facilitate the systematic entry of notes to PAF 2.2, for example 'Hot Notes' and 'NoteTool'. PAF3.0 can have a note or source for any event, and has changed the emphasis for lines starting with an exclamation mark - they are now called "shared notes".

6.5.3 Note records

Some genealogy packages put notes into separate records. Sometimes this is an installation option, with provision for using a word processor to maintain the notes. In GEDCOM exported from PAF 3.0 all notes are in separate records. The example below shows a note about a source document. The source consulted is the microfilm of the census enumerator's book, but to find the reference I used an index prepared and published by Lincolnshire Family History Society, so I added a note to say so.

```
0 @S6@ SOUR
1 AUTH Registrar General
1 TITL 1871 census St. Swithin, Lincoln
1 PUBL on microfilm by Public Record Office
1 REPO @R1@
2 CALN RG10/3372
1 NOTE @T3@
0 @T3@ NOTE indexed by Lincs FHS, in published book/microfiche
```

In the source record, the note appears as a reference:

```
1 NOTE @T3@
```

This points to the note record - which in this case is just one line:

```
0 @T3@ NOTE indexed by Lincs FHS, in published book/microfiche
```

In other packages using GEDCOM 5.5 this could appear all as one line within the source record:

```
1 NOTE indexed by Lincs FHS, in published book/microfiche
```

6.6 Adoption, fostering, etc

Some genealogy packages had provision for adoption and fostering before they were included in the GEDCOM standard, and the draft standards changed in this area, so there is considerable variety in the way this is shown in GEDCOM files. In the GEDCOM 5.5 standard, adoption is shown can be shown as an individual event, which can also show which parent adopted the individual, with values HUSB, WIFE, or BOTH. An example of the structure is:

```
1 ADOP
2 FAMC @F82@
3 ADOP HUSB
2 DATE 1927
2 NOTE Adopted by step-father
```

Adoption can also be shown as one of several child-to-family links in an individual record. Each can be followed by tag PEDI (pedigree) to show the relationship. PEDI can have values adopted, birth, foster, or sealing. An example for an individual fostered in family F83 and adopted by family F84 is:

```
1 FAMC @F83@
2 PEDI foster
1 FAMC @F84@
2 PEDI adopted
```

6.7 Associated individuals

The tag ASSO for Associated is used within an individual record to show how the submitter is related to the individual, or how some other unrelated individual is associated. The example below shows that Jemima Doe, submitter (U1) of the file, is great-niece of John Doe; and individual I52, William Roe, is executor of the will of John Doe.

```
0 INDI
1 @I10@ NAME John /Doe/
1 ASSO @U1@
2 TYPE SUBM
2 RELA Great-niece
1 ASSO @I52@
2 TYPE INDI
2 RELA Executor of will
0 INDI @I52@
1 NAME William /Roe/
0 @U1@ SUBM
1 NAME Jemima /Doe/
```

6.8 Role in event

Particularly where the individual is not the principal person in a documented event, it is necessary to show how the person appears. For example if an occupation is known from the daughter's marriage certificate, this could appear as:

```
1 OCCU Silversmith
2 SOUR @S92@
3 EVEN MARR
3 ROLE (Father of bride)
```

6.9 Terminators

The terminator marking the end of each line is specified to be a Carriage Return character (CR, ASCII character 0D in hexadecimal), optionally followed by a Line Feed character (LF, ASCII character 0A hex).

GEDCOM exported from Personal Ancestral File on IBM PC compatible computers with MS-DOS inserts CR and LF at the end of each line. The same is true of all other implementations I have seen, with one important exception: GEDCOM exported from the early versions of FamilySearch (IGI and Ancestral File on CD-ROM) has Carriage Return only as terminator. You are only likely to encounter this if you have IGI downloads made a few years ago - the current version of FamilySearch uses CR with LF as terminator.

6.10 Character Set

Accented characters and special symbols including the pound sign may give problems when moving a GEDCOM file from one system to another. The GEDCOM standard provides a way of identifying the character set in use. Be aware that the standard has been changed in this area; some GEDCOM implementations ignore changes of character set, some use sets no longer included in the GEDCOM 5.5 standard.

The GEDCOM standard says that the preferred character set is ANSEL (American National Standard for Extended Latin Alphabet Coded Character Set for Bibliographic Use), the same as the ALA (American Library Association) character set and MARC character set. ANSEL is a character set in which an accented letter is built from the normal code for the letter preceded by a non-spacing code for the accent or diacritic. For example, é (e acute) is code 226 (acute accent) followed by code 101 (letter e). GEDCOM provides for a change from ANSEL to the normal character sets of personal computers, where some accented letters are represented by a single code. For example in the IBM PC character set é is code 130. On an Apple Macintosh é is code 142. Microsoft Windows uses the ANSI character set in which é is code 233, so on an IBM PC there is even a difference between the character sets for Windows applications and non-Windows applications. Unicode (ISO 10646) is a character set under development which uses two and four byte sequences to represent latin (including accents) and non-latin character sets including Russian, Greek, Hebrew, Korean, Chinese and Japanese.

There is a difference between Versions of the GEDCOM standard in this area: version 3 numbers the sets 001 for ANSEL and 002 for ASCII, version 4 uses the names ANSEL IBMPC ASCII MACINTOSH and ANSI. Version 5.5 uses the names ASCII, ANSEL and UNICODE; it specifically prohibits use of the IBMPC set because the codes used depend on the code table setting in the exporting computer.

To change the character set for the whole transmission, include in the header a line with level 1, tag CHAR, value the number or name of the character set. For example to announce that a file from Family Tree Maker for Windows (FTW) destined for Ancestral File (ANSTFILE) uses the ANSEL character set, the header should include:

```
0 HEAD
1 SOUR FTW
1 DEST ANSTFILE
1 CHAR ANSEL
```

If Greek letters appear when you display a GEDCOM file using a word processor on an IBM PC, it is probably an ANSEL file with accents. For example an acute accent appears as a capital gamma (Γ).

All of these character conversions are done on characters with codes over 127, outside the ASCII and ISO 7-bit character set. There is provision in ISO standards for national characters at some codes below 127. A familiar example to UK users is the swapping of the $ (dollar), # (hash, number symbol) and £ (pound sterling); keyboards, displays, software and printers can often be set to change these around.

In GEDCOM the symbol @ (commercial at) has special significance in cross-reference indicators, pointers and escape sequences. An @ symbol in the text of a note is replaced in the GEDCOM file by two @ symbols together (@@).

Some packages generate only one character set - PAF 3.0 generates ANSEL, Family Origins version 5 generates ANSI. Others give a choice - Family Tree Maker version 5 gives a choice of ANSI, ANSEL, IBMPC, or MACINTOSH. Often packages recognise several variants on import - even if a GEDCOM file seems to have odd characters when viewed in a word processor it may behave perfectly on import into a package. If exporting, the safest choice is ANSEL.

A shareware program called ANSL2TXT to convert ANSEL to text for 7-bit ASCII, MSDOS or Windows code sets by Barney Tyrwhitt-Drake is available from Drake Software, registration £3 - address 1 Wychwood Rise, Great Missenden, Bucks HP16 0HB; phone 01494 862564, email barney@tdrake.demon.co.uk,
Web address http://www.tdrake.demon.co.uk/

6.11 Multimedia - OBJE objects and BLOB binary data

Many genealogy packages can include photographs in family trees, and can also associate sound or video recordings with an individual. GEDCOM 5.5 provides ways of transferring such multimedia information. One way is to provide a linkage from the individual or event to an external file, for example:

```
1 NAME Samuel /Hawgood/
1 OBJE
2 FORM gif
2 TITL Studio portrait of Samuel Hawgood about 1866
2 FILE c:\photos\IMG0027.gif
```

The other way is to embed the multimedia file within the GEDCOM file. This involves encoding the binary file to avoid control characters, and also involves breaking the binary file into object records no larger than 32 kilobytes. It involves object records with tag OBJE, and containing a binary object tag BLOB followed by a series of continuation lines with tag CONT, which will be an apparently meaningless jumble of up to 64 characters per line. The method of doing all this is specified in the GEDCOM 5.5 standard.

7. LIST OF ALL TAGS IN GEDCOM 5.5

This Chapter lists all tags in the GEDCOM 5.5 standard.

ABBR Abbreviation: used within a source record for the abbreviated name of the source document

ADDR Address: for event, attribute, submitter, or after SOUR in header; lines of address can have CONT (continuation) tags, or ADR1, ADR2, CITY, CTRY, STAE, POST - but not by PHON, which is at same level as ADDR

ADR1 Address line 1: follows ADDR

ADR2 Address line 2: follows ADDR

ADOP	Adoption: individual event qualified to show the adopting family, see page 32.
AFN	Ancestral File Number: reference number in individual record
AGE	Age: follows an event; for family event structure shows whether it is for husband or wife, see page 30.
AGNC	Agency: in event detail, or in source record following DATA
ALIA	Alias: cross-reference from an individual record, see page 27
ANCE	Ancestors: in submission record, shows number of generations of ancestors
ANCI	Ancestor Interest: cross-reference from individual record, pointing at a submitter record
ANUL	Annulment: family event
ASSO	Associates: in individual record, with structure showing type of association
AUTH	Author: in source record
BAPL	LDS Baptism: LDS Ordinance
BAPM	Baptism: individual event
BARM	Bar Mitzvah: individual event
BASM	Bas Mitzvah: individual event
BIRT	Birth: individual event; can be followed by FAMC to show the birth family when a child is also in a foster or adopted family
BLES	Blessing: individual event
BLOB	Binary Object data: in OBJE record for multimedia
BURI	Burial: individual event
CALN	Call Number: in source record following REPO and a cross-reference
CAST	Caste: individual attribute
CAUS	Cause: in event detail
CENS	Census: family event or individual event
CHAN	Change: can occur in most record types, followed by date and time record was changed, usually generated automatically
CHAR	Character set: in header record
CHIL	Child: in family record with pointer to individual
CHR	Christening: individual event
CHRA	Adult Christening: individual event
CITY	City: follows ADDR
CONC	Concatenation: follows NOTE or TEXT to show more text following without a line break.
CONF	Confirmation: individual event
CONL	LDS Confirmation: LDS Ordinance
CONT	Continued: follows NOTE or TEXT to show more text following on a new line, with a line break
COPR	Copyright: in header record
CORP	Corporate: in header following SOUR
CREM	Cremation: individual event
CTRY	Country: follows ADDR
DATA	Data: in source record or in source citation
DATE	Date: in event detail and many other places
DEAT	Death: individual event
DESC	Descendants: in submission record to show number of generations of descendants
DESI	Descendant Interest: cross-reference from individual record, pointing at a submitter record

DEST Destination: in header record to show which receiving system the GEDCOM is designed for
DIV Divorce: family event
DIVF Filing for Divorce: family event
DSCR Physical Description: individual attribute
EDUC Education: individual attribute
EMIG Emigration: individual event
ENDL LDS Endowment: LDS Ordinance
ENGA Engagement: family event
EVEN Event: family event or individual event, must be qualified by TYPE
FAM Family: starts family record
FAMC Family as child: in individual record with cross-reference to family record
FAMF Family file: in submission record
FAMS Family as spouse: in individual record with cross-reference to family record
FCOM First communion: individual event
FILE File: in header record, followed by name of the GEDCOM file
FORM Format: in header to show format of GEDCOM, in an object record to show format of multimedia, with PLAC to show which levels of placename are included.
GEDC GEDCOM: in header, followed by version number of GEDCOM standard
GIVN Given Name: follows NAME in individual record
GRAD Graduation: individual event
HEAD Header: start of header record
HUSB Husband: in family record with pointer to individual, also after AGE in a family event
IDNO Identity Number: individual attribute, should be qualified by TYPE
IMMI Immigration: individual event
INDI Individual: start of individual record
LANG Language: in header or submission record
LEGA Legatee: in individual record (structure is not clear from standard)
MARB Banns of Marriage: family event
MARC Marriage contract: family event
MARL Marriage licence: family event
MARR Marriage: family event
MARS Marriage settlement: family event
MEDI Media: in source record following CALN
NAME Name: in individual or submitter or repository records
NATI Nationality: individual attribute
NATU Naturalisation: individual event
NCHI Number of children: individual attribute
NICK Nickname: in individual record, follows NAME
NMR Number of marriages: individual attribute
NOTE Note: can start a NOTE record or follow many other tags
NPFX Name prefix: in individual record, follows NAME tag
OBJE Object: starts an object (multimedia) record
OCCU Occupation: individual attribute
ORDI Ordinance: in submission record, applies to LDS ordinances
ORDN Ordination: individual event
PAGE Page: following a source cross-reference, to show position within the source.

PEDI Pedigree: follows FAMC in an individual record to show type of family relationship, eg fostering or adoption

PHON Phone number: at same level as ADDR, for event, attribute, submitter, or after SOUR in header

PLAC Place: in event detail; in header followed by FORM to show place hierarchy

POST Postal code: follows ADDR

PROB Probate: individual event

PROP Property: individual attribute

PUBL Publication: in source record

QUAY Quality of data: in source citation, see page 20

REFN Reference number: user-allocated reference number in family, individual, repository, source, or multimedia object record

RELA Relationship: follows ASSO,

RELI Religion: individual attribute

REPO Repository: start of repository record or cross-reference to one

RESI Residence: individual attribute

RESN Restriction notice: in individual record, may appear in downloads from Ancestral File, either to show privacy or to show a record locked because there are conflicting views about the ancestry of an individual.

RETI Retirement: individual event

RFN Record File Number: in individual or submitter records

RIN Record Identity Number: in any type of record, applies to the record number allocated automatically by the computer system

ROLE Role: within source citation after EVEN

SEX Sex: in individual record

SLGC LDS Sealing to Child: LDS Ordinance

SLGS LDS Sealing to Spouse: LDS Ordinance

SOUR Source: start of source record, or with cross-reference to one

SPFX Surname prefix: follows NAME tag

SSN Social Security Number: individual attribute

STAE State: follows ADDR

STAT Status: used for LDS events

SUBM Submitter: starts a submitter record, or with cross-reference to one

SUBN Submission: starts a submission record, or with cross-reference to one

SURN Surname: follows NAME tag

TEMP LDS Temple: in submission record or LDS event

TEXT Text: in source record, or following a SOUR tag

TIME Time: follows a DATE

TITL Title: individual attribute (at same level as NAME, not subsidiary to it

TRLR Trailer: record at end of a GEDCOM file

TYPE Type: used after EVEN or ASSO or REFN to show the type of event or association or reference number

VERS Version: in header record to show version of GEDCOM, also to show version of SOUR system

WIFE Wife: in family record with cross-reference to individual

WILL Will: individual event

8. GEDCOM VERSIONS 1 AND 2

8.1 GEDCOM Version 1

GEDCOM version 1 was never widely used for transfer between packages. It was used for splitting and merging databases in the package Family History System. It has also been used for moving data from an early version of a package to a later version of the same package. You can recognise GEDCOM version 1 by two-character tags like BP for Birth Place.

8.2 GEDCOM Version 2 as implemented in PAF 2.0

You can recognise PAF 2.0 GEDCOM from the 8-digit dates and use of tags PARE, OLD, YOUNG and SIBL.

In GEDCOM version 2 (PAF version 2.0) dates have digits YYYYMMDD, with zeros for unknown month and day numbers. The digits can be followed by a single letter qualifier:

```
20 July 1837        18370720
About 1850          18500000A
Before Nov 1920     19201100B
After 3 Nov 1920    19201103F
```

Non-standard dates were preceded by N, dual dates were preceded by D:

```
See Notes           NSEENOTES
1 Feb 1738/9        D1738/17390201
```

8.2 Family Structure in PAF 2.0

You are unlikely to need to work out a family structure from a PAF 2.0 GEDCOM file, which is just as well; it is rather complicated. The representation of the family structure reflects that used within Personal Ancestral File. A family record has pointers to the husband, wife, and youngest child. An individual record has pointers to the family of the person's parents, the family in which the person is a spouse, and the individual who is the next older sibling in the family.

If a husband or wife has another marriage this is shown by a tag OTHE followed by a pointer to the other family: in the example below person 23 Samuel Hawgood is husband in family 106 and family 114. I used PAF 2.0 on an Amstrad PCW computer with CP/M. When I bought an IBM-compatible PC I used GEDCOM to transfer data about my family; the extracts below are from that file. The display screen shows the family of Samuel Hawgood as it appeared after import to PAF 2.2 on a PC. The GEDCOM is the file which was exported from PAF 2.0 on the Amstrad PCW.

If you have GEDCOM from an Amstrad PCW, or other GEDCOM needing conversion to a later standard, it may help you to know that a conversion service is available from Mrs Jeanne Bunting, Horseshoe Lane, Ash Vale, nr Aldershot, Hants GU12 5LL, phone 01252 325644, email firgrove@Compuserve.com.

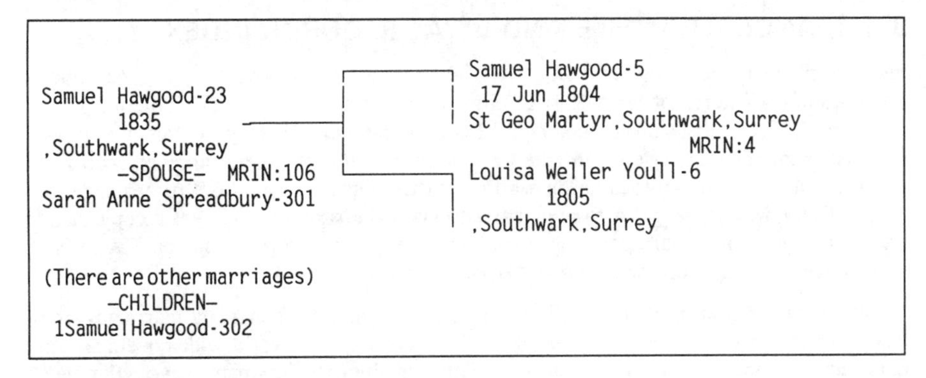

Display screen after import to PAF 2.2

File exported from PAF 2.0: extracts for family shown above

```
0 @23@INDI
1 NAME Samuel /Hawgood/
1 SEX M
1 BIRT
2 DATE 18350000
2 PLAC ,Southwark,Surrey
1 SIBL
2 OLD @22@                    (RIN of his older sibling)
1 FAMI
2 RFN @106@                   (One family in which she is a spouse)
1 PARE
2 RFN @4@                     (His parent's family)

0 @301@INDI
1 NAME Sarah Anne /Spreadbury/
1 SEX F
1 FAMI
2 RFN @106@                   (One family in which he is a spouse)

0 @302@INDI
1 NAME Samuel /Hawgood/
1 SEX M
1 FAMI
2 RFN @107@                   (One family in which he is a spouse)
1 PARE
2 RFN @106@                   (His parent's family)

0 @303@INDI
1 NAME Louisa /Hawgood/
1 SEX F
1 SIBL
2 OLD @302@                   (RIN of her older sibling)
1 PARE
2 RFN @106@                   (Her parent's family)

0 @106@FAMI
1 HUSB
2 RFN @23@                    (RIN of husband)
2 OTHE @114@             (Another family in which he is husband)
1 WIFE
2 RFN @301@                   (RIN of wife)
1 CHIL
2 YOUN @303@             (RIN of youngest child in this family)
```

9. IGI, ANCESTRAL FILE AND VITAL RECORDS INDEX

The International Genealogical Index (IGI) and Ancestral File are major genealogical databases of the Church of Jesus Christ of Latter Day Saints. They are available for public access on CD-ROM disks on computers in LDS Church Family History Centres: the system is called FamilySearch. Users can take away copies of IGI or Ancestral File records by printing them or by down-loading onto a floppy disk, either as an ASCII print image file or as GEDCOM. If you get a file from CD-ROM make sure you also get a copy of the LDS explanatory material about the use of the file on your own computer. There is a detailed description in my book *IGI in Computer* (ref 8).

The IGI contains transcripts of source records; for example baptisms and marriages from many parish registers. There are over 280 million records, with world-wide coverage. The microfiche edition of the IGI has been available in libraries for many years. For most countries there is a separate set of fiche sheets for each county or equivalent, with entries sorted by surname, forename and date. On the CD-ROM edition you can find all people of similar names within a country in one search.

The Ancestral File is a collection of pedigrees; it contains over ten million names. The first to be stored were derived from Family Group Sheets sent in by LDS church members. Users of several genealogy packages are now sending pedigrees in GEDCOM format on floppy disks to the LDS church.

IGI records down-loaded from CD-ROM in GEDCOM format are organised for ease of import to lineage-linked genealogy packages like Personal Ancestral File. Each IGI event produces separate records for one, two or three individuals. It also produces a family (marriage) record to link them, unless there is only one person named in the event.

When you import an IGI GEDCOM file into a genealogy package, the result is lots of little families. In a christening the child appears with date and place of christening; there is a note containing the batch number and LDS library call number for the source document, but only if you ask for source information. The father generally appears with forenames and surname only. The mother generally appears with forenames only.

In the IGI a name or a place can be up to 90 characters long in total. There is no limit on the length of a forename, surname or place name so long as the total does not exceed 90. As some packages limit the lengths of names, some IGI information cannot be transferred into its proper place. There is a particular feature which may make the "surname" longer than you would expect: any alternative surname is added to the first with the word "OR", e.g."BLACKBURN OR HATTERSLEY". Different packages deal with long names in different ways, and you should look at the manual for your package to find out what is done.

The Vital Records Index contains records similar to those in the IGI, but is being issued by the LDS Church as CDROM disks available for public sale.

9.1 Ancestral File on CD-ROM

The Ancestral File is a collection of pedigrees. The information on births, christenings, marriages, deaths, and burials is in the same format as in GEDCOM exported from Personal Ancestral File. However, as with the IGI, forenames, surnames and the individual parts of place names can be over 16 characters. In addition, each person with known ancestors has a unique "Ancestral File Number"; in the GEDCOM record this follows a tag AFN, e.g in a line "1 AFN 3QGV-1S".

9.2 Input to Ancestral File

The Family History Department of the LDS church nominally only accepts submissions to Ancestral File from genealogy packages they have checked and approved. There are requirements and recommendations about the form in which the information is entered; details should be in the manual for the genealogy packages. The LDS Church publish a leaflet "FamilySearch - Contributing Information to Ancestral File", Ref 4. In practice the LDS Church seem to welcome a GEDCOM file from any package as a submission to Ancestral File; it helps them if placenames have the country included.

Lance J Jacob (Ref 5) gives helpful information about submissions to Ancestral File. Make sure you copy only the part of your database you want included. Make sure your name and address gets into the file (in the "Submitter" record). Follow the manual for your package about Ancestral File submission, which is different from preparing a GEDCOM file for other purposes. Think before looking at the file with a word processor; it is easy to allow unwanted control characters to be introduced when saving from a word processor.

9.3 Other databases in FamilySearch

FamilySearch includes databases of Social Security Death Information (USA, 1937 on), and the (US) Military Index of deaths in the Korean and Vietnam wars. Be careful if you use them, "place of issuance" or "home of residence" are put into the "birthplace" fields.

9.4 Vital Records Index

The LDS Church has transcribed and indexed many records which have not been added to the IGI. These are now being issued on CDROM for public sale as the Vital Records Index. On your computer at home you can print, copy in Rich Text Format (RTF), or copy records in PAF 3 (GEDCOM 5.5) format. The listing on page 42 is the record for one individual, the family record for his marriage, and the source record referenced. It adopts a "belt and braces" approach to the source reference - the microfilm number 1067128 within the Family History Library of the LDS Church is given three times - but surprisingly none of the references has a tag CALN for "call number". The source record gives the dates of coverage of the register on this microfilm, and of other registers for the same parish.

Notice that the citation text in the family record gives the names of the husband and wife and of both their fathers. Included in the GEDCOM file (but not in the figure) are individual records for these, and family records linking them to their children. So the GEDCOM file from this event gives four individual records, three family records, a source record, and is linked to a repository record - always that for the LDS Family History Library in Salt Lake City. The source citation and source record follow the GEDCOM 5.5 structure described in Chapter 4.

```
0 @I405557-1@ INDI
1 NAME Arthur /Hawgood/
2 GIVN Arthur
2 SURN Hawgood
1 SEX M
1 FAMS @F405557-1@
1 FAMC @F405557-2@
1 SOUR @SM017283@
2 PAGE FHL Number 1067128
2 NOTE Husband in Marriage Extract for Arthur HAWGOOD and Priscilla HUMPHRY
2 DATA
3 DATE FROM 1859 TO 1862

0 @F405557-1@ FAM
1 HUSB @I405557-1@
1 WIFE @I405557-2@
1 MARR
2 DATE 9 Jan 1862
2 PLAC Saint Nicholas, Brighton, Sussex, England
1 SOUR @SM017283@
2 PAGE FHL Number 1067128
2 NOTE Marriage Extract for Arthur HAWGOOD and Priscilla HUMPHRY
2 DATA
3 TEXT Extract: Vital Records Index - British Isles
4 CONT Marriage event for:
4 CONT Husband: Arthur HAWGOOD
4 CONT Wife: Priscilla HUMPHRY
4 CONT Marriage Date: 9 Jan 1862
4 CONT Recorded in: Saint Nicholas, Brighton, Sussex, England
4 CONT Husband's Father: Samuel HAWGOOD
4 CONT Wife's Father: Richard HUMPHRY
4 CONT Source: FHL Number 1067128   Dates: 1859-1862
3 DATE FROM 1859 TO 1862

0 @SM017283@ SOUR
1 AUTH The Church of Jesus Christ of Latter-day Saints
1 PUBL Vital Records Index - British Isles, CDs, 1998
1 REPO @R1@
1 TITL Brighton, St. Nicholas, Sussex, England (Extracted records)
1 NOTE Source: Vital Records Index - British Isles
2 CONT Event Type: Marriage
2 CONT Recorded in: Brighton, St. Nicholas, Sussex, England
2 CONT Reference: FHL 1067104     1731-1761
2 CONT Reference: FHL 1067105     1755-1797
2 CONT Reference: FHL 1067106     1797-1813
2 CONT Reference: FHL 1067128     1859-1862
2 CONT Reference: FHL 1067129     1862-1865
2 CONT Reference: FHL 1067130     1865-1868
2 CONT Reference: FHL 1067131     1868-1872
2 CONT Reference: FHL 1067169     1872-1881
```

Individual, family and source records from Vital Records Index

10. TRANSFERS BETWEEN PACKAGES

Import

Back up your family records before using GEDCOM to add to them. So far I have never seen a GEDCOM import fail, but I have made mistakes myself -once I added the new people to the wrong family entirely. But I recovered quickly from my back up copies.

When you receive a file, first import it into an empty database. Note any messages displayed during the import. Look at any exception listing. Some packages (eg PAF 3) have a choice of either generating an exception listing, or putting the exceptions into notes for the individuals concerned.

If there are many exceptions, it may be worth finding a friend who has a recent version of a package from the same developer. For example, if you have a GEDCOM version 4 file from Roots III, you should be able to import it into Ultimate Family Tree. You would then be able to export it from Ultimate Family Tree in GEDCOM 5.5 format.

If you decide to look at the GEDCOM file and work out what information has not transferred, make a copy of the GEDCOM file and work on the copy. This avoids any risk of disrupting the GEDCOM file you have received.

Editing information for import

It is always worth trying a GEDCOM import to an empty database before you start editing the file; it may reveal unsuspected problems, or it may work better than you expect. Software developers do try to allow for known features of other packages in their import utilities. If you have Internet access, it is worth contacting the software developer by email. The GEDCOM problem you are trying to solve may be well known, and the developer may have standard advice or even a small program to enable you to import the information.
The simplest way to replace any missing information is to edit the records in the new database, and type the information as notes, or transfer information from the word processor to the genealogy package by using Windows copy and paste. Make sure you check it carefully after entering it.

If you are adept at editing files, it is more accurate and may be quicker to make systematic edits to the GEDCOM file. You can use any text editor or word processor which can output an ASCII file with no control characters except Carriage Returns and Line Feeds at the ends of lines. For example use Windows WordPad, save as "text document". You may have to be careful about character sets when doing this, particularly if there are accented or other special characters in the GEDCOM file.

The easiest changes are the replacement of single extra fields by notes. For example in GEDCOM from Roots III, change every line starting "1 ILLE" to "1 NOTE Illegitimate. Roots III used GEDCOM version 4 with many extra tags; ILLE is one of the tags that is not in the GEDCOM 5.5 standard.

It is also easy to remove leading exclamation marks in notes, which have special meanings in PAF but not in other packages. Change "1 NOTE !" to "1 NOTE ". Similarly you can remove leading commas from places; change "2 PLAC ," to "2 PLAC ". If you make these changes, the reports you produce for the other members of the family will look more sensible, without odd punctuation; but be aware that the changes will affect any subsequent GEDCOM transfer back into PAF.

I find that many users of computers for genealogy perform quite complicated transformations on data to avoid the time taken and errors produced in retyping. The suggestions in this section are intended to help these transformations.

Export

When exporting information to send to another genealogist, try to restrict the export to the people of interest. It is easier to select descendants of one person or ancestors of one person when exporting than when importing. It is also quicker importing a small file. If your recipient has problems importing your file it may be possible to generate it again, but make different choices when exporting. The simplest files in GEDCOM 5.5 format are those destined for PAF 3.0 and Ancestral File. The simplest files in GEDCOM 3/4 format are those destined for PAF 2.1 to 2.31. You will probably end up with a great deal of your information in notes, but at least it will transfer easily.

REFERENCES

1. "The GEDCOM Standard" Release 4.0 August 1989. The GEDCOM standards and specifications are written and published by the Family History Department, Church of Jesus Christ of Latter Day Saints, 50 East North Temple Street, Salt Lake City, Utah 84150, USA: they are available for a nominal fee. See Ref 7 for the current issue, Release 5.5
2. "Personal Ancestral File GEDCOM Specifications" January 25, 1990. Publisher as Ref 1, supplied with Ref 1.
3. "The GEDCOM Standard" Release 3. 9 Oct 1987. Publisher as Ref 1.
4. "FamilySearch - Contributing Information to Ancestral File", published in 1990 with several later versions. 4 page leaflet. Published by the Ancestral File Operations Unit (of the LDS Church), address as Ref 1. Available from Distribution Centres and Family History Centres of the LDS Church.
5. Lance J Jacob, "GEDCOM and a few Ancestral File pointers" "Genealogical Computing" Jan 91 pp 8,9,46. Practical information about submissions to Ancestral File.
6. "The GEDCOM Standard" Release 5. Several versions of Release 5 of the standard were published as drafts for comment - e.g. Release 5.2 dated 2 April 1993. Publisher as Ref 1.
7. "The GEDCOM Standard" Release 5.5. Publisher as Ref 1, published Dec 1995. For an electronic version of the GEDCOM Standard 5.5 see ftp site ftp://gedcom.org/pub/genealogy/gedcom
8. "IGI on Computer" by David Hawgood, 1998, published by the author, distributed by Family Tree Magazine, 61 Great Whyte, Ramsey, Huntingdon, Cambs PE17 1HL; phone 01487 814050, fax 01487 711361.

INDEX